Healing Grief

Healing Grief

Victor M. Parachin

Chalice Press.
St. Louis, Missouri

All Scripture quotations, unless otherwise noted, are taken from the *Holy Bible*, New Living Translation, copyright © 1996. Used by permission of Tyndale House Publishers, Inc., Wheaton, Illinois 60189, U.S.A. All rights reserved.

Scripture quotations marked (NIV) are taken from the HOLY BIBLE, NEW INTERNATIONAL VERSION®. NIV®. Copyright © 1973, 1978, 1984 by International Bible Society. Used by permission of Zondervan Publishing House. All rights reserved.

Cover photo: © D. Jeanene Tiner
Cover design: John L. Hurst, Jr.
Interior design: Elizabeth Wright
Art direction: Michael Domínguez

This book is printed on acid-free, recycled paper.

Visit Chalice Press on the World Wide Web at
www.chalicepress.com

10 9 8 7 6 5 4 3 2 1   01 02 03 04 05 06

Library of Congress Cataloging–in–Publication Data

Parachin, Victor M.
   Healing grief / Victor M. Parachin.
     p. cm.
   Includes bibliographical references.
   ISBN 0-8272-1441-3 (pbk. : alk. paper)
    1. Grief–Religious aspects–Christianity.   I. Title.
BV4905.2 .P28 2001
248.8'66—dc21   2001002355

Printed in the United States of America

Contents

Introduction

Death is a fact of life.

Sooner or later each one of us will lose, to death, someone we love, value, and hold dear. That loss will plunge us into mourning. While the pain of bereavement is as intense as any pain we will ever experience, we do have a choice in how we respond to the loss. We can experience a good mourning or we can experience a bad mourning. We can experience healing grief or remain frozen in time, stuck in a place of pain. The choice is ours. Sadly, there are some whose experience with loss results in bad mourning. They feel forever the oppressive hand of grief. Unable to move on, they remain riveted in one place, irrevocably attached to their disappointment, anger, remorse, regret, resentment, or guilt—or some combination of these. They are permanently doubled over from the blow of grief.

On the other hand, there are those—and they are the vast majority of grievers—who experience good mourning. They remember forever the one who has died, but come to terms with the loss and find new ways of living without the loved one. Those who experience good mourning find themselves enlarged in heart, spirit, and mind. For them, mourning becomes the raw material out of which they forge a new life and deepen their personality, becoming more aware, more compassionate, more loving, more gentle, more insightful, and more wise.

This is a book about healing grief. You have picked up this book because you have had a loss to death and because you want to heal, to recover, to move forward. Today the choice is yours—a good mourning or a bad mourning, healing or hurting. Resolve now that you *will* move through grief, that you will eventually arrive in a better place despite the magnitude of your loss.

Perhaps this story can be instructive. During World War II the British had a small military force in Singapore. When it became clear that the Japanese had military superiority and could easily take over Singapore, the British surrendered. All British military became Japanese prisoners of war (POWs). One officer, however, entertained the idea of slipping out of the city to take his chances in the jungle.

However, he had two conflicting sources of information about life in the Malaysian jungle. Some people told him that the jungle was an extremely dangerous place filled with wild animals, deadly snakes, and fruit so poisonous that one bite of it would result in instant death. Yet others told the officer that the jungle was a most hospitable place. It offered ample fresh water and a wide variety of delicious wild fruit. The jungle was a safe place and could sustain human life indefinitely, they said.

After considering both viewpoints, the officer decided not to become a POW, choosing to take his chances in the jungle. He did survive and eventually made his way to friendly forces who reunited him with the British military. However, he came to his own unique conclusion about the jungle. The jungle, he told friends, was neutral. It was not out to destroy him nor to support him. *To survive he had to make wise use of the environment around him.*

That officer's experience sheds light on the journey through grief. Life is not out to destroy us nor to simply support us. *Life is neutral!* Surviving the burden of loss means we have to make wise use of the environment around us. What follows in this small book are ten steps you can take to experience healing grief.

STEP ONE

HEALING GRIEF

Know What to Expect

Expect the unexpected.

The loss of a loved one throws people into an emotional jungle. The psychological geography is unknown, unfamiliar, and uncomfortable. You may be amazed and frightened by the powerful and sometimes conflicting emotions that will roll over you in the days and weeks and months following a death. Sometimes simply knowing the roller coaster emotions that can come is helpful in alleviating some of the stress. Following are some of the most common symptoms that people experience as a part of grief. As you read them, keep in mind that you may not experience all the symptoms, nor do they progress in any particular order. Because every loss is unique, every mourner grieves in his or her own unique way.

Shock and denial—"This can't be happening to me!" The initial information that a death has occurred is shocking and numbing. The full impact of the tragedy will take some time to be realized. This is God's way of protecting us from the immediate and full impact of the loss. In a way, shock and numbness give us space and time to gradually absorb the magnitude of the loss.

Loneliness and vulnerability— *"I didn't know loneliness could hurt so much."* When the funeral service is over, family and friends leave us and return to their own daily activities. It is at that time that loneliness and feelings of vulnerability overwhelm us. One woman, who lost a child, recalls: "My daughter's death is the loneliest of all experiences I have ever had. I had no idea that loneliness could be so deep and intense. I also find myself hovering over the other two children, worrying about every little detail. One death in the family has left me feeling so very vulnerable."

Tears and weeping— *"I just can't stop crying."* People who have never cried throughout their adult lives suddenly find themselves weeping at any time. Be reassured that tears are a normal and healthy response to death. Tears are nature's "safety valves." They cleanse the body of toxins that build up from stress, and provide an important release of tension.

Pain and hurt— *"I don't think I can take any more!"* The loss of a loved one conspires with other emotions to create deep psychological pain. In her book *Barbara Bush: A Memoir,* the former first lady includes a chapter on her daughter Robin, who died from leukemia at three years of age. Mrs. Bush writes that the funeral started "the most painful period of adjusting to life after Robin. We (she and her husband George) wakened night after night in great physical pain—it hurt that much."[1] Although it may seem unbearable, the pain will lessen in intensity over time.

Panic and anxiety—*"What am I going to do?"* A death brings with it a great many changes. Income may be reduced, and financial instability can become a daily struggle. You may become a single parent having to juggle your work, your children, their schooling, and extra activities without a partner's help. Or you may become a widow or widower finding that your circle of friends has changed, with some unable to relate to you the way they did when you were part of a couple. All this creates feelings of anxiety and even panic at times.

Guilt and regret—*"I should have done more."* Like many grievers, you may find yourself second-guessing your words and actions: *If only I had been there. If only I hadn't said that. If only I had called.* This way of thinking results in feelings of guilt and regret. Challenge your thinking, because a closer examination will usually reveal that you did your best under the circumstances.

Anger and frustration—*"How could she do this to me?"* One man, whose wife died from cancer at thirty-five years of age, found himself angry with her after the death. "She had smoked for nearly twenty years. Even though she was well aware of the studies about the dangers of smoking, she never quit. There are times when I become angry that she let this happen to herself and to me!" You too may find yourself angry and frustrated—at the person who died, at a member of the medical staff, or at some insensitive family member or friend. A death triggers bouts of anger from time to time.

Depression and sadness— *"Will life ever be worth living again?"* Although depression is not a welcome experience, it is a normal one to have following a death. It is also a beneficial one. In his book *Death and Grief: A Guide For Clergy,* Alan D. Wolfelt notes: "Depression is nature's way of allowing for a time-out while one works to heal the wounds of grief. Depression shuts down the physiological system and prevents major organ systems from being damaged."[2]

Recovery and readjustment— *"Knowing I am adjusting to life again would please my loved one."* The time will come when you will be free of pain and depression over the loss of a loved one. Rather than bringing you to the verge of tears, memories of your loved one will bring you a smile. In his book *Grief Counseling and Grief Therapy,* J. William Worden writes:

> One benchmark of a completed grief reaction is when the person is able to think of the deceased without pain. There is always a sense of sadness when you think of someone you have loved and lost, but it is a different kind of sadness—it lacks the wrenching quality it previously had. One can think of the deceased without physical manifestations such as intense crying or feeling a tightness in the chest.[3]

STEP TWO

HEALING GRIEF

Put Your Pain into Words

Your suffering will spill over into words.

Don't deny yourself the opportunity to express your feelings. Shakespeare had it right when he wrote: "Give sorrow words; the grief that does not speak / Whispers the o'er-fraught heart, and bids it break" (*Macbeth* 4.3.209). One way to get your pain into words is by speaking with those who can listen compassionately without judging you or what you say. Talking is good therapy. The term *therapist* comes from the Greek word *therapeo*. That Greek word can mean either 'listening' or 'healing.' In fact, in some ancient Greek manuscripts where the word *therapeo* is used it is unclear whether what is being described is listening or healing. Listening and healing are interconnected concepts. Every time we express our feelings, a layer of pain is removed.

Consider this insight from writer Lois Duncan. Her 18-year-old-daughter, Kaitlyn, was killed, the victim of what police termed a "random shooting." What most helped Lois and her husband, Don, deal with their horrific loss were people who simply listened. "The people we found most comforting made no attempt to distract us from our grief," she says. "Instead they encouraged Don and me to describe each excruciating detail of our nightmare experience over and over. That repetition diffused the intensity of our agony and made it possible for us to start the healing."[4]

If you are the kind of person for whom privacy is important and who prefers not to speak with others about inner turmoil, another option is to write out your feelings and thoughts. The simple act of such writing in a journal for as little as fifteen minutes produces emotional healing. A study conducted at the University of Miami demonstrated that two sessions of writing were equally effective as two sessions of psychotherapy.

One who has documented that writing is a means of healing is James W. Pennebaker, professor of psychology at Southern Methodist University. Using students from the university, Dr. Pennebaker evaluated each participant's health status according to the number of illness visits each student made to the university health center in the months before and after the writing experiment. Dr. Pennebaker divided the student volunteers into two groups, both of whom agreed to write for about 15 minutes each day for four consecutive days. One group agreed to simply write about superficial topics. The other wrote about personal traumatic experiences, which included childhood sexual abuse, suicide attempts, parental abandonment, and the death of a parent or sibling. In many cases, the student had never discussed the trauma with anyone.

Not surprisingly, writing about trauma initially made people feel worse. However, at the six-month follow-up, Dr. Pennebaker found that the most dramatic drop in number of illness visits to the university health center was among those who wrote about their deepest thoughts and feelings surrounding the trauma. Blood tests were given to participants in order to measure the health effects of writing. An evaluation of those blood tests revealed there were significantly higher levels of T-cells (known to help fight infections and virus) among those who wrote about their traumas.

The lesson: Put your pain into words.

STEP THREE

HEALING GRIEF

Let Friends Be Your Lifeline

Sorrow shared is sorrow diminished.

A small circle of good friends can make a big difference. This is recognized in the Bible—"Two people can accomplish more than twice as much as one…If one person falls, the other can reach out and help. But people who are alone when they fall are in real trouble" (Ecclesiastes 4:9–10).

There is healing power in friendship, so reach out. Consider this wisdom from noted grief authority Rabbi Earl A. Grollman. In *What Helped Me When My Loved One Died,* he writes:

> The common denominator of grief is loneliness. A special person—your loved one—can no longer share your life. You are bereft, alone. Talk to a friend. Share your feelings. Let the right people know that you need support and feedback. They cannot bring you comfort unless you allow them to enter your sorrow.[5]

Rabbi Grollman speaks of turning to the "right people." It is important you identify those who will encourage, support, and empathize with you. Then, stay in their company. Generally, the "right people" for grievers include those who listen compassionately and without judgment and who respond with these kinds of empathy statements:

- ▲ This must be very difficult for you.
- ▲ This has got to be hard to accept.
- ▲ What can I do? How can I help?
- ▲ I'm so sorry.
- ▲ Tell me more.
- ▲ It's okay to cry.
- ▲ Call me whenever you want to talk.
- ▲ You are in my thoughts and prayers.

Compassionate listeners do more listening than speaking. They never make you feel as though you have been judged or misunderstood. *You know that they know your pain* or, at the very least, are trying hard to understand and be supportive. Blanket yourself with these kinds of good people. They will help stabilize you. If you worry about being "too depressing" or "too bothersome" for your friends, a good technique is to expand your circle of supports. That way you are not burdening one or two people. I learned of this approach when a young woman called me. She explained that her cancer had recurred and was spreading rapidly. The woman, a social worker and therapist herself, knew she needed to talk with others about her condition, but did not want to overload her husband and close friends. So she was reaching out and had identified several others she felt would be open to her and would listen compassionately. She asked if I would be willing to be part of that circle and, of course, I was pleased to be included in her expanded company of supporters.

STEP FOUR

HEALING GRIEF

Be Aware of "Miserable Comforters"

Words can heal or hurt, inspire or injure.

Some people are clumsy when trying to be helpful. An advice columnist received an irate letter from a woman who had recently lost her husband. The grieving widow was infuriated by a neighbor who came to the funeral and said to her: "I know how you feel. We lost our dog two months ago and we're still mourning."

Since step three advises you to stay in the company of helpful people, step four is the "flip-side": Limit your time with people who are not helpful or who are even hurtful. The fact is that some people just don't understand the complexity of bereavement and grief recovery. Rather than being sympathetic, these people are judgmental of you. They don't listen patiently, and they interrupt you, offering advice on how you should be feeling, what you should be saying and thinking, how you should be living your life. These types of people have been around for a long time. They are "miserable comforters," according to biblical character

Job, who had to deal with such people. After various tragedies came his way, including the death of several family members, "friends" came to "comfort" Job. However, they really came filled with their own notions of how Job ought to be responding. Exasperated at all their talk, Job finally declared: "What miserable comforters you are! Won't you ever stop your flow of foolish words?" (Job 16:2–3).

People who are miserable comforters often use these kinds of clichés:

- ▲ I know how you feel. (They usually don't unless they've had a loss themselves.)
- ▲ She/he led a full life.
- ▲ At least you had 20/30/40 years together.
- ▲ You're young; you can have other children.
- ▲ You're young; you can marry again.
- ▲ It was God's will.
- ▲ God needed your (son/daughter/husband/ father) in heaven.
- ▲ Your loved one is now one of God's angels.

If we look carefully at the above kinds of statements made by miserable comforters, it is clear the issue is not whether what they say is true or false. It may be true that "he led a full life" or that "you can marry again." The issue is insensitivity to pain, because those statements convey the idea that the loss is not that significant. The problem with the clichés used by miserable comforters is that they minimize your loss. It is almost as though the miserable comforters are saying: "What's the big deal? He led a full life." Or "What's the big deal? You can marry again." While remaining civil, try to keep your distance from people who say such things, as they will only cause you confusion and hurt.

However, there is one more thought to consider about people who are miserable comforters. Sometimes it is possible to educate and inform them about grief, thereby transforming them into helpful people. As a griever you should feel free to correct and inform them when their comments or actions are off the mark. A Zen Buddhist story illustrates this point:

As two sisters returned from their mother's funeral, one sister said, "I'm angry with you!"

"Why?" asked her sister.

"Because you didn't act appropriately at the funeral."

"What do you mean?" the sister asked.

"You seemed to be having too much of a good time," the sister lamented.

"Well, I was having a good time."

"How can you act that way with mother dead only a few days?" the sister almost shouted.

(Here comes the educating and informing part of the dialogue.)

"I think sorrow and joy run on parallel paths like two horses pulling the same wagon. The important thing is to recognize each in its place and in its time."

The sister's wisdom made an impression on the sister who was upset. The upset sister simply responded:

"But you were laughing so much and…"

"Sure, I found joy in seeing old friends. I loved talking with them about mother and reliving happy memories. The grieving I do on my own. If I seemed happy, I was—in that moment. And I liked the food that was brought."

"But what about appearance, how all that looked to others?" the sister asked.

"Appearances are your problem, not mine."

Again, the accusing sister softened her words and thoughts, admitting: "You are right about the food, though."

"I'm right about the joy too," her sister responded.

STEP FIVE

HEALING GRIEF

Commit to Overcoming

We suffer, but we can overcome our suffering.

In his book *A Gift of Hope,* Robert Veninga, a professor at the University of Minnesota, tells of parking his car one freezing January morning and trudging through the snow toward his office. "I found myself preoccupied with disquieting thoughts. The icy winds cut through my parka. Winter never seemed more brutal. To make matters worse, six hours of nonstop teaching were on the agenda, coupled with four hours of committee meetings." As his mind darted from one negative perception to another, Dr. Veninga found himself extremely tense as he approached his office.

Briefly he took his eyes off the icy sidewalk and looked up. In front of him was the Masonic Cancer Center at the University of Minnesota. To his astonishment, he saw a large sign in a patient's window: "I need a large sausage pizza!" "A smile came to my face," he recalls. "Here was a patient, possibly living out the last days of life, who had retained a sense of humor."

Rather suddenly, Dr. Veninga's problems did not seem so great. Throughout the day his mind kept going back to the sign and the patient. Finally, out of curiosity, he called the nursing station on that floor and asked whether the nurse had seen the pizza sign. "Oh yes. You ought to meet that patient. He has one of the most virulent forms of cancer, but his spirit is amazing. He just won't give up." Dr. Veninga could not resist asking: "Did anyone bring him a pizza?" The reply: "By noon his room was lined from door to window with large sausage pizzas. We had enough pizza to feed everyone in the unit." [6]

There is an important lesson in this story that every griever needs to learn. It is a lesson about overcoming. It is a lesson about battling back against the oppressive pressure of bereavement. It is a lesson about pushing away the darkness. Commit to overcoming bereavement. Minister and psychologist Ann Kaiser Stearns has interviewed and studied survivors from all sorts of tragedies—people whose lives were shattered by disease, death, chronic pain, and being prisoners of war. In her book *Coming Back: Rebuilding Lives After Crisis and Loss,* she cites the following as attitudes crucial for overcoming adversity:

- ▲ I will not be defeated.
- ▲ I will vividly examine the future.
- ▲ I will take advantage of available opportunities.
- ▲ I will not assume the victim posture.
- ▲ I will accept life's challenges.
- ▲ I can do it if I set my mind to it.
- ▲ I have to be willing to expand.
- ▲ I will find a way to get what I want.

▲ I am consciously deciding to be in the company of good people.[7]

Study this list carefully. Make these your attitudes as you manage mourning. And when facing discouragement or even despair over your circumstances, keep in mind the truth that *attitudes are more important than the facts*. The story is told of a beginning teacher in Illinois who loved her first-year experience as a teacher. Because the principal had not visited her classroom to evaluate her teaching skills, she assumed her contract would not be renewed for an additional year.

At the end of the school year she packed up her personal material and prepared to say goodbye to students and colleagues. The principal saw her, smiled, and said, "We have enjoyed having you here this year and look forward to having you teach with us again next year!" The woman was astonished and replied, "Well, I haven't received a contract to teach next year, so I just assumed you thought I had done a poor job and didn't want me back."

However, the principal reassured her, saying, "We really want you back. Your students scored higher on their achievement tests than any of our other students in the last ten years. You've got to come back next year." Deflecting the compliment, the teacher said, "It's easy to teach when you have such a great group of kids as I had. They were sharp, interested, motivated, and all of them had IQs of 150, 152, 153, and even higher."

The principal asked how she knew the students possessed such high IQ scores. She cited the materials he had given her at the beginning of the school year, which contained a sheet of paper with the students' names and IQ scores on it. The principal smiled at her and said: "Those were their locker numbers."

There is an important lesson in that story: Because she believed the students had high IQ scores, the teacher treated them and taught them as though they were highly intelligent, creative, and motivated young people. Her attitude was one that demanded high-level, quality work. She had great expectations and backed those up with a belief that the students could rise to the academic challenge and accomplish their work.

That teacher's experience powerfully illustrates this truth: *Attitudes are more important than facts.* Those who are grieving should think about that truth—*attitudes are more important than facts.* The fact is that you have lost a loved one to death. The grief is hard, and the journey is lonely. Yet your attitude can triumph over the facts about loss. Adopt the attitude that you will overcome, that you will transform pain into gain, that you will become an enlarged person as a result of this hard experience.

STEP SIX

HEALING GRIEF

Tap into Your Faith

Death raises profound spiritual issues.

Tap into your faith, and you will gain comfort, support, strength, insight, wisdom, and a sense of direction. If you have not been in the habit of actively participating in a faith community, bereavement is a very good time to seek one out. One of the impacts of losing a loved one to death is fear—fear of the future and fear in the present. The greatest antidote to fear is faith.

- ▲ Where fear imprisons, faith liberates.
- ▲ Where fear paralyzes, faith motivates.
- ▲ Where fear disheartens, faith encourages.
- ▲ Where fear sickens, faith heals.
- ▲ Where fear leaves us hopeless, faith generates hope.

This contemporary saying has much wisdom and truth in it: "Fear knocked at the door. Faith answered. No one was there!"

During your time of bereavement it is important that you turn to a spiritual leader—one who has gifts of listening, empathy, compassion, and some experience with grief. That person can become an invaluable ally for you. Also, during your time of bereavement, take advantage of the spiritual opportunities your house of worship offers—Bible study groups, fellowship, worship, quiet and meditation, prayer, music. All these can be great sources of comfort and healing.

As you journey through grief, connect with God, our "unseen partner" in life. Here are seven Bible texts to help you connect and remain connected:

1. Know that God cares—1 Peter 5:7.
   Give all your worries and cares to God, for God cares about what happens to you.

2. God is with you in grief—Isaiah 43:1–2.
   The LORD who created you says, "Do not be afraid, for…I have called you by name; you are mine. When you go through deep waters and great trouble, I will be with you. When you go through rivers of difficulty, you will not drown!"

3. God will heal you from the wound of grief—Psalm 147:3 and Psalm 34:18.
   He heals the brokenhearted, binding up their wounds.
   The Lord is close to the brokenhearted;
   he rescues those who are crushed in spirit.

4. God is the source of comfort when we hurt—2 Corinthians 1:3–4a.
   All praise to the God and Father of our Lord Jesus Christ. He is the source of every mercy and the God who comforts us. He comforts us in all our troubles.

5. By connecting to the Christ spirit, you will overcome—John 16:33.
   "Here on earth you will have many trials and sorrows. But take heart, because I have overcome the world."

6. God is leading you to a good future—Jeremiah 29:11.
   "For I know the plans I have for you," says the LORD. *"They are plans for good and not for disaster, to give you a future and a hope."*

7. God will renew and restore you—Hosea 2:14.
   "I will...transform the Valley of Trouble into a gateway of hope."

The death of someone we love creates one of life's most difficult challenges. Yet God is powerfully present to help us deal with such large losses. Consider the prayer written by Archibald Campbell Tait, a nineteenth-century Archbishop of Canterbury. Between March 11 and April 8, 1856, Tait and his wife lost five of their six daughters to scarlet fever. His prayer is powerful in its affirmation of God's goodness in the presence of great pain.

O God, you have dealt very mysteriously with us. We have been passing through deep waters; our feet were well-nigh gone. But though you slay us, yet will we trust in you...They are gone from us...You have reclaimed the lent jewels. Yet, O Lord, shall I not thank you for now? I will thank you not only for the children you have left to us, but for those you have reclaimed. I thank you for the blessing of the last ten years, and for all the sweet memories of these lives...I thank you for the full assurance that each has gone to the arms of the Good Shepherd, whom each loved according to the capacity of her years. I thank you for the bright hopes of a happy reunion, when we shall meet to part no more. O Lord, for Jesus Christ's sake, comfort our desolate hearts. May we be a united family in heart through the communion of saints; through Jesus Christ our Lord. Amen.[8]

So whether you follow the tenets of Judaism, Christianity, Islam, Hinduism, or Buddhism, tap into your faith. Whether your spiritual tradition is from the East or the West or the New Age Movement, tap into it. It will sustain you, enlarge you, and restore you.

STEP SEVEN

HEALING GRIEF

Get Physical

Physical exercise lifts the spirit, eases stress, and alleviates depression.

The truth is that a weakened body can lead to a weakened mind and spirit. A variety of recent studies consistently demonstrate that people who exercise regularly (at least thirty minutes a day, five days a week) are less likely to be depressed, and they enjoy better physical health. According to James Blumenthal, professor of medical psychology at Duke University, "For some clinically depressed patients, exercise is as effective as the best medications we have."[9] The positive effect of exercise is long-lasting as well. One study showed that those who exercised regularly for nearly twenty years were one and a half times less likely to become depressed as those who exercised sporadically. Exercise is a way of doing something positive for yourself. It is a way of taking control of an area of your life. These often constitute important steps in breaking the cycle of depression.

Every bereaved person should take on some physical activity, because depression is a common emotional state following a loss to death. Study after study demonstrates that exercise is effective in reducing and eliminating depression. A recent study published in the Archives of Internal Medicine revealed that regular exercise lifts depression just as well as prescription antidepressants. For the study, researchers split 156 men and women with major depressive disorder into three groups.

One group exercised aerobically for forty minutes three times a week. Another group took a prescription antidepressant. A third group both exercised and took medication. After sixteen weeks, all groups had made significant improvement. While those who took medication had faster initial responses, exercise soothed depressive symptoms just as effectively as medication in the long run.[10]

Even if you have not been exercising regularly, this is a good time to begin taking a daily walk, jogging, biking, swimming, skating, and so forth. Some find it easier to exercise regularly by joining a club where they are motivated by the presence of others working out. The key is to find a physical activity that you can enjoy and then do it for thirty minutes a day, at least five days per week. If you are concerned about your physical ability to take on exercise, consult with your physician. Then begin lightly and gradually and work toward picking up the intensity of your activity.

STEP EIGHT

HEALING GRIEF

Become Informed

Knowledge is power.

The more you know about grief and bereavement issues, the more power you will have over your life. During the last twenty years there has been a proliferation of exceptional books published about grief recovery. You should take the time to find some of those and read them. The information you gain will empower you because you will come to understand more clearly the issues that emerge from loss. In all likelihood, you will come to understand that your journey—while it feels tumultuous—is quite normal for anyone who has had a loss to death. Visit your library or bookstore and scan the list of books they offer. Select some and begin your own study in bereavement.

Some good books that I often recommend to grievers include the following:

Colgrove, Melba, Harold H. Bloomfield, and Peter McWilliams. *How to Survive the Loss of a Love*. New York: Bantam Books, 1983.

Grollman, Earl A., comp. *What Helped Me When My Loved One Died.* Boston: Beacon Press, 1981.

————. *Living When a Loved One Has Died.* Boston: Beacon Press, 1997.

James, John W., and Frank Cherry. *The Grief Recovery Handbook: A Step-by-Step Program for Moving Beyond Loss.* New York: Harper & Row, 1988.

Lightner, Candy, and Nancy Hathaway. *Giving Sorrow Words: How to Cope with Grief and Get On with Your Life.* New York: Warner Books, 1990.

Parachin, Victor M. *Grief Relief.* St. Louis: Chalice Press, 1991.

Schiff, Harriet Sarnoff. *The Bereaved Parent.* New York: Penguin Books, 1978.

Shaw, Eva. *What to Do When a Loved One Dies: A Practical Guide to Dealing with Death on Life's Terms.* Irvine, Calif.: Dickens Press, 1994.

Stearns, Ann Kaiser. *Living through Personal Crisis.* Chicago: Thomas More Press, 1984.

STEP NINE

HEALING GRIEF

Join a Support Group

The sharing of sadness is a catalyst for healing.

Grief support groups can be found in virtually every community. Take the time to locate one and participate. Here is a list of benefits cited by the bereaved themselves after they joined a support group:

- ▲ I found people who really understood what I was going through.
- ▲ I saw people successfully coping with grief. They became role models.
- ▲ It was a place where I made some new and very good friends.
- ▲ I could cry, and no one made me feel like I was abnormal.
- ▲ I realized I was not the only one suffering from grief.
- ▲ Hearing from others about their losses somehow comforted me.
- ▲ My support group nurtured in me a deep sense of hope for the future.
- ▲ I found myself being able to help others through the group.

- ▲ My depression eased greatly.
- ▲ I began to feel better physically.
- ▲ It gave me a social activity that I looked forward to each week.
- ▲ I find people not only surviving but thriving.

To find a group in your area, inquire of your spiritual leader, funeral director, local hospital, or the telephone yellow pages under a Mental Health listing.

STEP TEN

HEALING GRIEF

Be Patient

You will heal, but the healing comes slowly, gradually.

The most common complaints I hear while leading grief support groups are those concerning pressures the bereaved feel to be well. Many family members and friends seem to feel that after ten or twelve months the bereaved should be back to normal. Often they pressure the bereaved to recover by making comments such as these:

- ▲ It's been nearly a year now. Don't you think you should be over this?
- ▲ She/he has been gone a year. When are you going to start dating?
- ▲ It's been twelve months now. I think you're feeling sorry for yourself.

The fact is that most people need between two and four years to make a complete recovery from grief. When it comes to the loss of a spouse, some therapists suggest that it takes one month of recovery for every year of the marriage. Thus, if you had been married twenty-five years, you might need twenty-five months to make the adjustment. If you lose a child, the recovery time is even longer. These are some comments I've heard in grief support groups about recovery and the time frame:

- ▲ "It took me four years until I was no longer consumed by loss on a daily basis."
- ▲ "One night, about a thousand sunsets after my daughter's death, I realized that my heart was no longer raw and bleeding. There are scars, but the pain is finally easing."
- ▲ "After my husband died, I quit baking. Suddenly, after about three years, I woke up one morning and felt I wanted to bake bread. I knew then that I was on the road to recovery and adjustment."

This is the lesson from those comments: Don't let people pressure you. There is no quick fix for grief. Your wound will heal, but the healing will be very gradual. So be patient with yourself and ask others to bear with you.

Especially for Men

Eight Steps Men Can Take to Heal from the Wound of Grief

After a naval career that spanned nearly twenty-five years, Bernard and Jeanne eagerly anticipated life together after military retirement. However, just a few months after Bernard retired, Jeanne was diagnosed with cancer and died thirteen months later. "Over the course of our marriage, we had endured many separations because of sea duty. Retirement was to be our time to make up," Bernard sadly tells a friend. "Now that Jeanne is gone, I'm plagued with troubling thoughts: Who am I without her? We were married nearly three decades. She was the stabilizing person in my life. Here I am 56 and alone. For the first time in my life I'm very unsure of myself," he laments.

The death of a person we love is one of life's harshest blows. The bereavement that follows is often a lonely, torturous, frightening journey. And that journey from grief to healing is frequently more acute for men than women because social networks are designed to deliver rapid support to women while men are approached more slowly and less directly. Yet men, like women, can and do recover. Here are eight steps that men can take to heal from the wound of grief:

Step 1. Become informed about grief. Visit a library or bookstore and select books about bereavement and grief issues. Read everything you can about the grieving process. The information you read will empower and encourage you. "Books were my lifeline," says one recent widower. "I set aside a weekly day to make a trip to the library. There I carefully selected books that would inform or inspire me. The books were not only successful in touching my heart and inspiring me to continue on, but they normalized the grieving process for me. By reading about bereavement of others, I quickly learned that my emotional reactions were quite normal and that I wasn't going crazy."

Step 2. Express and explore your feelings. Slipping into denial can happen when men suppress feelings. Do not "keep a stiff upper lip," "take it like a man," or put up any stoic front for people. Instead, express and explore the wide gamut of uncomfortable feelings that will roll over you—feelings such as guilt, regret, anger, depression, loneliness, despair. Robert DiGiulio says that after an accident claimed the lives of his wife, daughter, and in-laws, "I discovered that it does no good to fight such feelings. Pushing them down only seems to make them come back with even greater fury. Instead, I had to learn to respect these feelings as part of me—a testimony to my intense love and loss."[11] Only when DiGiulio was able to accept and even embrace those feelings as a natural and normal part of the grieving process was he able to work through them, he says.

Step 3. Maintain links with people. Don't be the "Lone Ranger." Bereavement is an isolating experience. Loneliness becomes acute because your beloved partner has died. Do not complicate the bereavement by being the "Lone Ranger." Reach out to trusted family and friends. Here is sound advice from Candy Lightner and Nancy Hathaway, authors of *Giving Sorrow Words:*

> Discuss your feelings with other people. It's not sufficient to recognize them yourself; it's better to share them. Spend time with supportive people, not only because it helps in reducing loneliness but also because those people can help put your feelings into perspective. Talking about your feelings with someone who is willing to listen can be enormously consoling, especially if that person has experienced a death similar to the one you are grieving.[12]

Step 4. Step away from gender stereotypes. Some men will grieve much the same way women are permitted to grieve—by expressive sharing and showing of feelings. Other men, however, will be less expressive. Don't make value judgments about yourself. Grieve in your own unique way. Respect the grieving patterns that you are establishing and get others to support you on that path. To guide your bereavement journey, consider these adaptive grieving styles that therapists say characterize masculine grievers:

- ▲ Shelving thoughts and feelings in order to meet pressing personal and professional obligations, and then dealing with them when appropriate
- ▲ Opting for active ways of expressing grief, such as physical exercise, competitive sports, hobbies
- ▲ Seeking companionship in lieu of support
- ▲ Using withdrawal and solitude as a way of reflecting, understanding, and adapting
- ▲ Writing in a journal as a way of tracking progress through grief

Step 5. Expect and accept emotional turmoil. "All my life I've been emotionally steady. My children refer to me as the family 'Rock of Gibraltar.' But since Karen's death six months ago, I feel like an emotional basket case," says Kenneth, a Midwest engineer. "For no apparent reason, I can well up with tears. I am easily frustrated and anger quickly. I can't seem to concentrate or focus well." The reality is that the death of a loved one often unleashes many unfamiliar and uncomfortable emotions. There can be shock, disbelief, numbness, guilt, regret, anger, loneliness, vulnerability, tears, panic, anxiety, and intense sadness. Many grievers are unable to sleep well and find their appetite is harshly curbed. Expect this emotional turmoil and accept the reactions as a normal and natural part of grieving. Remind yourself that the emotional storm will pass.

Step 6. Commit to adapting and adjusting. During World War II, a young American lieutenant was stationed in England. The bomber bases, hacked out of the sodden English countryside, were seas of mud. "On the ground, people were cold, miserable, homesick. In the air, people were getting shot. Replacements were few; morale was low," the man recalls.

However, there was one sergeant—a crew chief—who was always cheerful, always good-humored, always smiling. The lieutenant was intrigued by his positive attitude and observed him one day as the sergeant struggled in a freezing rain to salvage a plane that had skidded off the runway into an apparently bottomless mire. He was whistling cheerfully. "Sergeant, how can you whistle in a mess like this?" the man asked. The sergeant gave him a mud-caked grin, saying: "Lieutenant, when the facts won't budge, you have to bend your attitudes to fit the facts. That's all there is to it."

The sergeant's words are good advice for grieving men: *When the facts won't budge, you have to bend your attitude to fit the facts.* Because we cannot reverse the painful loss of a loved one to death, we must adapt and adjust our attitudes in order to manage and grow through the grief process.

Step 7. Get physical. Exercise is the "best" antidepressant available. That is the opinion of Harvard-educated physician Dr. Andrew Weil, M.D. and author of several best-selling books. "Aerobic exercise is actually the best antidepressant I know, provided it is done vigorously enough and often enough," Weil says. "In addition to its many well-known effects on the body, it increases production of endorphins, the brain's own opiate-like molecules that are associated with some of our best natural highs."[13] Dr. Weil advises thirty minutes of sustained aerobic activity at least five days a week to gain the maximum benefit from exercise. The effort must be great enough to get the heart rate up, accelerate breathing, and cause perspiration.

Step 8. Give yourself ample time to heal. Despite your best efforts, the process of adjustment and recovery is a slow, agonizing one. There may be weeks at a time when you are unable to discern any progress. Be assured, however, that you are gradually healing. Be patient with yourself. Do not place too much pressure on yourself to heal rapidly. "Give yourself time to move through grief at your own pace in your own individual way," advises DiGiulio. He also offers this personal insight: "My wife's death thrust me into new, awkward roles and responsibilities. I tried not to expect too much of myself too soon, just to start with the small tasks first, to be patient with myself and my mistakes. I discovered that the routine tasks of maintaining my job and family helped restore in my life that familiar structure which the chaos of grief threatened to destroy."[14]

By taking these steps you, as a man, ensure that you will have a healthy bereavement and that you will complete the grief process. Like others before you, you will make the transition from anxiety to acceptance and from pain to peace. You will, in fact, heal from the deep wound of grief.

Nine Common Myths and Realities about Grief

Writing to an advice columnist, a woman expresses these concerns about family members who are grieving a loss due to death:

> My brother and his wife lost a teenage son in an auto accident six months ago. Of course this is a terrible loss, but I worry they're not working hard enough to get on with their lives. This was God's will. There's nothing to do about it. The family has been patient and supportive, but now we're beginning to wonder how long this will last and whether we may not have done the right thing with them.

That woman's concern is shaped by a faulty understanding about bereavement. She, like many others, has neither an informed understanding nor accurate information about the grieving process. The woman incorrectly assumes that grief is of short duration, ends within a specific time frame, and is the "will of God."

Whenever there is a loss to death—spouse, parent, child, sibling, grandparent—grievers struggle with a variety of confusing and conflicting emotions. Too often their struggle is further complicated by well-meaning individuals who say and do the wrong things because they are untutored about the bereavement process.

Here are nine of the most common statements people either believe about grief or offer to those who are grieving, the myths that underlie them, and the corresponding realities about actual grief. Knowledge of these issues is extremely helpful for both the bereaved and those who want to help them. The bereaved can gain assurance that their responses to death are quite normal and natural. Simultaneously, family, friends, religious leaders, and other caregivers can have correct information about grief, thus enabling them to respond more patiently, compassionately, and wisely.

"It's been a year since your spouse died. Don't you think you should be dating by now?"

MYTH: A new relationship can simply substitute for the old one.

REALITY: It is impossible simply to "replace" a loved one. Susan Arlen, a New Jersey physician, offers this insight: "Human beings are not goldfish. We do not flush them down the toilet and go out and look for replacements. Each relationship is unique, and it takes a very long time to build a relationship of love. It also takes a very long time to say good-bye, and until good-bye really has been said, it is impossible to move on to a new relationship that will be complete and satisfying."[15]

"It was the will of God."

MYTH: God somehow directly intends every death in the way that it occurs.

REALITY: The Bible makes this important distinction: Life provides minimal protection, but God provides maximum support. One example of that truth is this statement from Jesus: "In this world you will have trouble. But take heart! I have overcome the world" (John 16:33, NIV). Calling a tragic loss the will of God can have a devastating impact on the faith of others. Consider this woman's experience:

> I was nine years old when my mother died, and I was very, very sad. I did not join in the saying of prayers at my parochial school. Noticing that I was not participating in the spiritual exercise, the teacher called me aside and asked what was wrong. I told her my mother died and I missed her, to which she replied: "It was the will of God. God needs your mother in heaven." This made me very angry with her and with God because I felt I needed my mother far more than God needed her. For years I was angry with God because I felt he took her from me.

When statements of faith are made, they should focus on God's love, support, and comfort. Rather than declaring it was the will of God, a better response is to gently suggest: "God is with you in your pain." "God will help you day by day." "God will guide you through this difficult time." When seeking to deliver spiritual comfort to the bereaved, take your cue from this biblical text: "God has said, 'Never will I leave you; never will I forsake you'" (Hebrews 13:5, NIV). Also, rather than talking about God's "taking" a loved one, it is more theologically accurate to place the focus on God's "receiving and welcoming" a loved one.

"You look so well."

MYTH: Outward appearance accurately expresses inner emotions.

REALITY: The bereaved do look like the nonbereaved on the outside. However, on the interior, feeling level, they experience a wide range of chaotic emotions—shock, numbness, anger, disbelief, betrayal, rage, regret, remorse, guilt. These feelings are intense and confusing. C. S. Lewis wrote shortly after the death of his wife: "In grief, nothing stays put. One keeps on emerging from a phase, but it always recurs. Round and round. Everything repeats. Am I going in circles, or dare I hope I'm on a spiral? But if a spiral, am I going up or down it?"[16] In reality, though the bereaved may "look well," they may, in fact, be struggling greatly with managing their emotions and feelings. Thus, when people comment in astonishment, "You look so well," grievers feel misunderstood and further isolated. A more helpful response is to simply and quietly acknowledge their pain and suffering through statements like these: "This must be very difficult for you." "I am so sorry!" "How can I help?" "Is there anything I can do?" "Would you like to talk?"

"It's been six (or nine or twelve) months now. Don't you think you should be over it?"

MYTH: Everyone heals from grief by the same timetable.

REALITY: There is no rapid healing for the pain of bereavement. Of course grievers wish they could be over it in six months. But grief is a deep wound that takes a long time to heal. The exact time frame differs from person to person. Glen Davidson, professor of psychiatry and thanatology at Southern Illinois University School of Medicine tracked 1,200 mourners. His research revealed an average recovery time of eighteen to twenty-four months.

"You need to get out more and be more active."

MYTH: Keeping yourself active speeds up the healing process.

REALITY: Encouraging the bereaved to maintain their social, civic, and religious ties is healthy. Grievers should not withdraw completely and isolate themselves from others. However, it is not helpful to pass judgment on the bereaved and pressure them into excessive activity. Erroneously, some caregivers try to help the grieving "escape" from their grief through such excessive activity. There is no escape from grief, and too much activity only delays the recovery process. Consider this lament from a woman whose husband had died seven months earlier:

> Several of my friends who have not experienced grief firsthand have been pressuring me to "get out more and get active." They say, solemnly, "What you must do is get out among people, take a cruise, travel abroad. Then you won't feel so lonely." My feeling is their advice would simply interrupt my grieving, not bring it to an end. I've now developed a standard response for their advice: "I am not lonely for the presence of people; I am lonely for the presence of my husband." But how can I expect these innocents to understand that I feel as though my body has been torn apart and my soul has been mutilated? How could they understand that for the time being, life is simply a matter of day to day survival?

"Funerals are too expensive, and the services are too depressing."

MYTH: Funerals do not contribute anything of importance to the grieving process.

REALITY: Funeral costs vary greatly and can be managed by the family according to their preferences. More importantly, the funeral visitation, service, and ritual create a powerful therapeutic experience for the bereaved. In her book *What to Do When a Loved One Dies,* Eva Shaw writes:

A service, funeral or memorial, provides mourners with a place to express the feelings and emotions of grief. The service is a time to express those feelings, talk about the loved one, and begin the acceptance of death. The funeral brings together a community of mourners who can support each other through this difficult time. Many grief experts and those who counsel the grieving believe that a funeral or service is a necessary part of the healing process and those who have not had this opportunity may not face the death.[17]

"The best thing we can do (for the griever) is to avoid discussing the loss."

MYTH: Talking about the death only intensifies the wound and slows down the grieving process.

REALITY: The bereaved need and want to talk about the loss, including the most minute details connected to it. Grief shared is grief diminished. Each time a griever talks about the loss, a layer of pain is shed. "The people most helpful to us when our son, Mitchell, died were those who let us talk, talk, and talk about every detail of his life and death," recalls one bereaved father. "The best comforters were those who made no attempt to distract us from our grief, rather encouraging us to talk freely and from our heart. It was only through the expression of our feelings via words that the intense pain of loss began to ease."

"You're young; you can get married again" or *"Your loved one is no longer in pain now. Be thankful for that."*

MYTH: The belief that such statements help the bereaved.

REALITY: Clichés are seldom useful for the grieving and usually create more frustration for them. Avoid making any statements that minimize the loss, such as: "He's in a better place now." "You can have other children." "You'll find someone else to share your life with." It is more therapeutic to simply listen compassionately, say little, and do whatever you can to help ease burdens.

"She cries a lot. I'm concerned she is going to have a nervous breakdown."

MYTH: Excessive crying is a sign of unhealthy grieving.

REALITY: Tears are nature's safety valves. Crying washes away toxins from the body that are produced during trauma and crisis. That may be the reason so many people feel better after a good cry. "Crying discharges tension, the accumulation of feeling associated with whatever problem is causing the crying," says Frederic Flach, associate clinical professor of psychiatry at Cornell University Medical College in New York City. "Stress causes imbalance and crying restores balance. It relieves the central nervous system of tension. If we don't cry, the tension doesn't go away."[18] Caregivers should get comfortable at seeing tears from the bereaved and, perhaps, even cry with them.

Some Commonsense Answers about Grief

Recently I conducted two funerals in the space of one week. The first one was for a sixty-seven-year-old man who left behind a beloved wife, several children, and many grandchildren. The other was for a nine-month-old infant. Her parents found her dead in her crib.

Whenever there is a death, surviving family members enter the uncharted emotional territory of bereavement. Most people have limited experience or knowledge of what grief recovery entails. Whether the loss is that of a mature adult or that of a child, the ensuing grief is difficult and challenging. Here are answers to some of the most commonly asked questions by the bereaved about grieving:

Q: The pain of loss is unbearable. How long will it last?

A: Grief recovery cannot be rushed. There is no quick fix. Generally, grief recovery takes longer than most people assume. Healing normally takes from three to five years. This does not mean your pain will continue to be as intense as in the early months after the death.

What usually happens is that feelings of depression and sadness gradually melt away as grievers adjust to their loss and begin to reinvest energy in new relationships and opportunities. Try to be patient with your grief. It may help to recall the wisdom of the Roman philosopher Seneca: "Time heals what reason cannot."

Q: I am disappointed because my family and friends are not as supportive as I thought they would be. What can I do?

A: Unless someone has experienced a loss to death, he or she cannot truly understand the impact of grief. You can find understanding and acceptance in a support group where others are making a similar journey. A grief support group can also be inspiring because you will see other bereaved men and women successfully managing their feelings and moving forward. Another thing you can do is respond compassionately toward those who have disappointed you. In his book *Living with Loss, Healing with Hope,* Rabbi Earl A. Grollman reminds grievers not to be surprised if some friend shifts take place following a loss. "Times of tragedy can be a crucible in which friendships are tested. You may feel abandoned by certain friends who vanished even before the funeral, or after a token condolence call."[19] Rabbi Grollman softens this disappointment, reminding grievers that many people feel unequipped to help others through grief, and therefore they act in awkward and clumsy ways. "They (friends) may mistakenly think you want to be alone. They, too, are frightened by death. Try to forgive them," he urges. "After all, during these turbulent days there are many times you don't understand yourself."[20]

Q: It has been 14 months since my wife died, and I feel worse, not better. Is this normal?

A: Many people report that the second year of bereavement is more difficult than the first. There are many reasons for this, including the fact that people are numb and in shock during the first weeks and months after a death. Again, be patient and do not expect overnight recovery. Try reminding yourself that others have recovered from their grief, and you will too, in your own time.

Q: The loneliness I feel is excruciating. Can anything be done to help?

A: Loneliness is common to all who experience the death of a loved one. To help ease your loneliness, find a kind and compassionate friend who will listen and allow you to speak about your pain. Grief shared is grief diminished. Remember playwright William Shakespeare's sage advice, as quoted earlier: "Give sorrow words; the grief that does not speak / Whispers the o'er-fraught heart, and bids it break" (*Macbeth* 4.3.209).

Q: I dread the thought of upcoming holidays, anniversaries, birthdays, and other family events. How can I deal with these occasions?

A: Joyous occasions and holidays, such as Thanksgiving and Christmas, are especially hard for the bereaved because they tend to magnify the sense of loneliness after a loss. It is common for grievers to dread such times, but usually anticipation of the event is worse than the day itself. It is usually beneficial to participate in family celebrations and festivities because you will gain support and fellowship by interacting with family and friends, which can be more helpful than being alone.

Q: I can't sleep more than three or four hours at a time and constantly feel tired. Is this normal? Should I take medication to help me sleep?

A: What is called a "sleep disorder" is extremely common after a loss to death. However, prescription drugs and other numbing agents, such as alcohol, should be avoided. Sooner or later, your body will take over and allow you to rest properly. Meanwhile, avoid daytime naps. Curtail and regulate the amount of time you spend in bed. The more time spent in bed, the more fragmented your sleep becomes. Go to bed at a regular time and rise at the same hour each morning. Avoid lounging in bed.

Q: I can't stand being in this house anymore. It used to be a place of joy and peace but is now a depressing place because everything reminds me of my loved one who died. I want to move out. Is this a wise thing to do?

A: Unless there is a pressing financial need, you should not sell your home or move out in the first year after your loss. All major decisions should be postponed until after the period of intense grief. You need time for your feelings and grief to subside. Then evaluate how you truly feel about your house and other circumstances.

Q: I find myself crying easily at unexpected times. It embarrasses me. Is there anything I can do about my tears?

A: Tears are not a sign of weakness, but rather, a sign of love and natural pain. They testify to an important relationship's being ruptured by death. Crying is a natural response to loss. Also, tears have a health benefit in that they relieve the body of the stress caused by grief. That is why people often feel better after a good cry. Nineteenth-century British writer Albert Smith noted: "Tears are the safety-valves of the heart when too much pressure is laid on it."[21]

Q: I feel abandoned by God. Life seems so cruel and unfair. Does God know or care about me?

A: When a loved one dies, it is not unusual to feel abandoned by God. Remember that God understands and accepts your feelings, and loves you unconditionally. Your feelings of abandonment may be relieved by recalling the many biblical passages that reflect God's care for us through all life's circumstances. Some examples include: "The LORD remembers us, and he will surely bless us." (Psalm 115:12). "Give all your worries and cares to God, for he cares about what happens to you." (1 Peter 5:7). "He is the source of every mercy and the God who comforts us. He comforts us in all our troubles." (2 Corinthians 1:3–4) Pray that God will continue to heal and strengthen you daily.

Notes

STEP 1

[1]Barbara Bush, *Barbara Bush: A Memoir* (New York: Charles Scribner's Sons, 1994), 46.

[2]Alan D. Wolfelt, *Death and Grief: A Guide For Clergy* (Muncie, Ind.: Accelerated Development Publishers, 1988), 57.

[3]J. William Worden, *Grief Counseling and Grief Therapy: A Handbook for the Mental Health Practitioner* (New York: Springer Publishing Co., 1982), 16.

STEP 2

[4]Lois Duncan, "Helping Friends Who Grieve," *Woman's Day* (October 2, 1990): 29.

STEP 3

[5]Earl A. Grollman, *What Helped Me When My Loved One Died* (Boston: Beacon Press, 1981), 9.

STEP 5

[6]Robert Veninga, *A Gift of Hope: How We Survive Our Tragedies* (Boston: Little, Brown & Co., 1985), 224–25.

[7]Ann Kaiser Stearns, *Coming Back: Rebuilding Lives After Crisis and Loss* (New York: Random House, 1988), 255.

STEP 6

[8]Archibald Campbell Tait in *The Complete Book of Christian Prayer* (New York: Continuum, 1996), 96.

STEP 7

[9]James Blumenthal cited in "Feel Better Faster," *The Plain Truth* (March/April 1999): 29.

[10]Archives of Internal Medicine study cited in "Running Lifts Depression," *Runner's World* (March 2000): 19.

APPENDIX 1

[11]Robert DiGiulio, "Losing Someone Close," in *Care Notes* (St. Meinrad, Ind.: Abbey Press, 1996), 2.

[12]Candy Lightner and Nancy Hathaway, *Giving Sorrow Words: How to Cope with Grief and Get On with Your Life* (New York: Warner Books, 1990), 207.

[13]Andrew Weil in *Dr. Andrew Weil's Self Healing Newsletter,* Premier Issue, Summer 1999, 8.

[14]Robert DiGiulio, "Losing Someone Close," 5.

APPENDIX 2

[15]Susan Arlen, "Misconceptions and the Bereavment Experience," in *Bereavement Magazine,* September/October, 1994: 2.

[16]C. S. Lewis, *A Grief Observed* (New York: Bantam Books, 1961), 34.

[17]Eva Shaw, *What to Do When a Loved One Dies: A Practical Guide to Dealing with Death on Life's Terms* (Irving, Calif.: Dickens Press, 1994), 35.

[18]Frederic Flach, M.D. cited in *Emotions and Your Health,* Emrika Padus and eds. of *Prevention* (Emmaus, Pa.: Rodale Press, 1986): 142.

APPENDIX 3

[19]Earl A. Grollman, *Living with Loss, Healing with Hope: A Jewish Perspective* (Boston, Mass.: Beacon Press, 2000), 53.

[20]Ibid.

[21]Albert Smith, cited in *The New International Dictionary of Thoughts* (New York: Standard Book Company, 1954), 635.